BADGERS!

A MY INCREDIBLE WORLD PICTURE BOOK

MY INCREDIBLE WORLD

Copyright © 2023, My Incredible World

All rights reserved. This book or any portion thereof may not be reproduced or used in any manner whatsoever without the express written permission of the copyright holder.

www.myincredibleworld.com

Badgers are furry mammals that belong to the weasel family.

Badgers live in many parts of the world, including North America, Europe, and Asia.

They have distinct black, brown, and white striped patterns on their face and body.

Badgers range in size between 22 and 36 inches (56 - 91 cm) long.

Depending on the type of badger, they can weigh as much as 35 pounds (16 kg)!

Badgers are known for their incredibly strong digging abilities.

They use their sharp claws to create large, underground burrows called **setts.**

Badger burrows have different areas for sleeping, storing food, and raising young.

A family of badgers is called a **clan** or a **cete**.

Badgers are usually solitary, other than those taking care of babies.

Baby badgers are called **cubs** or **kits**.

Female badgers give birth to small litters of around 1 to 5 cubs in the spring.

They communicate with each other using vocalizations, body language, and scent markings.

Badgers are **omnivorous**, which means they eat both plants and other animals.

Their diet includes earthworms, snakes, mice and other rodents, and even some fruits.

Badgers have excellent senses of smell and hearing, which helps them locate food underground.

They are **nocturnal**, which means they are most active during the night.

Some badgers, like the American badger, team up with coyotes or foxes to hunt and catch prey!

When threatened, they can use their sharp claws and powerful jaws to defend themselves.

Badgers are amazingly clean animals.

Some even build shallow pits away from their living space to use as toilets!

Badgers are incredible!

Printed in Great Britain
by Amazon